Robert Paine Hudson

Songs of the Cumberlands

A series of poems descriptive of scenes and incidents among the

Cumberlands and throughout the South

Robert Paine Hudson

Songs of the Cumberlands
A series of poems descriptive of scenes and incidents among the Cumberlands and throughout the South

ISBN/EAN: 9783337213244

Printed in Europe, USA, Canada, Australia, Japan

Cover: Foto ©Thomas Meinert / pixelio.de

More available books at **www.hansebooks.com**

PRICE, TWENTY-FIVE CENTS.

SONGS

OF

THE CUMBERLANDS.

By ROBERT P. HUDSON,

Author of "Roving Footsteps," etc,

Ever truly,

Robert P. Hudson

SONGS

OF

THE CUMBERLANDS;

A SERIES OF POEMS DESCRIPTIVE OF

SCENES AND INCIDENTS AMONG THE CUMBERLANDS

AND THROUGHOUT THE SOUTH.

By ROBERT P. HUDSON,

Author of "Roving Footsteps," etc.

NASHVILLE, TENN.:
C. R. & H. H. HATCH, PUBLISHERS,
1887.

PROEM.

The Cumberlands, reaching through Kentucky, Tennessee, and North Georgia, have lately been justly celebrated in the stories of various prose writers, but never before have they appeared in song. It is hoped that this little volume is not misplaced in attempting to fill the vacancy thus existing.

The author wishes to say that these songs were not written with a view to publication, but were addressed to friends as his experiences in life. He has not made poesy a business, but a pastime. It is only after the toils of the field that he has had time to attend the flowers of his little garden. Whether, in his attempts on Parnassus, he has reached the court of Erato, the reader must say.

CONTENTS.

Songs of the Cumberlands.

WHENCE THESE SONGS?

"Whence these songs?" the children ask me,
  As they press their lips to mine ;
"Have you others?" yet they task me,—
  Little fairies half divine.

Youthful muses overtake me,
  When my country bursts to spring ;
Thousand happy voices make me
  Thrill with pleasure, so I sing.

Every spike that spreads its sweetness
  Where the loud-note song-ters throng;
Every mountain in its greatness,
  Whispers to my heart a song.

'Tis the music of the wildwood,
  That you read in rhythmic chimes,
'Tis the stories of my childhood
  Brought to me from olden times.

'Tis the lofty palms that greet me,
  And the voice of Southern seas ;
'Tis the children dear that meet me
  Everywhere, that give me these.

WHERE FOUNTAINS LEAP.

Where fountains leap and rivers laugh,
  O'er which soft shades as playful fleet,
And mountain peaks the heavens quaff,—
  Exults my heart, rebound my feet.

To-day I press the mountain's height,
  Mid golden beams, o'er streamlets free;
To morrow, where will fall my light?
  I'll laugh through vales, I'll kiss the sea.

But whether splendid art may gleam,
  Or gorgeous phase be pictured there,
Know first your beauteous face will beam,
  Your name be whispered first in prayer.

I love your mountains, love the sea,
  This glorious light mid vales I tread,
But love that lives with you and me
  Will be a sweeter radiance shed.

Oh! still as fondly truthful prove,
  This foretaste is not all we'll see;
But know, while bursts my heart with love,
  For you its sweetest pangs will be.

THE CANEY FORK.

(A tributary of the Cumberland.)

Crystal river, circling, seething,
Foaming river, babbling, moaning,
Pearly river, bright, reflecting.
Darkling river, oft defiant,
Giant river, now unwieldy,
Wild, deep river, yet so gentle,
Laughing river, ever happy,
Playful river, always pleading,
O my river of all rivers!
Clustered round your drowning cascades,
Filling, blessing all your waters,
Resting on your cliffs and mountains,
Live my dearest, sweetest memories.
        O my earliest friend and comfort,
I have spent so many summers
Wading, trolling in your rapids,
Rowing on your circling eddies,
Trod your vales from morn till evening,
Heard my voice from cliffs respondded,
Sheltered in your caves from tempests,
Swam your cooling tide by moonlight,
No, I never can forget you,
Never, never breaks my fondness.
        Flowery isles and rippling fountains,

"Towering rocks with deepest shadows,
Water-falls half hid with vapors."—Page 13.

Cloudless skies with balmy breezes,
Towering rocks with deepest shadows,
Water falls half hid with vapor,
Lovely girls that kiss you, bless you, —
Make your course a tour of rapture,
Most endeared of all the rivers,
Mimic sea, the heaven's mirror!

When through other lands I wander,
Though I meet with cliffs as lofty,
Water falls that speak as loudly, ¦
Yet I find me sighing, sighing,
For your rocky banks, my river!

In my heart enthroned forever,.
Time nor fate can e'er depose you,
Far though be my straying footsteps,
I will oft return to greet you,
Rest from cares that daily haunt me,
Shun a world of envy, censure,
View the sands my feet imprinted,
Seek your cliffs, my early shelter,
Plunge into your throbbing bosom,
Source of all my youthful pleasure,
O my river of all rivers!

LAUGHING SPRING.

Patient spring has suffered so
Waiting for the frosts to go,
Moved at last the hoary fields
She ! er gentle influence yields ;
Waked to life each forest rings,
Earth the brightest verdure brings,
Sold to joy I seek the wood,
Trillums, vines obstruct the road,
Lucid leaves shut out the sky,
Brooklets mumble, zeph\ rs sigh ;
Through each dear, secluded grove
Follow me if spring you love!
Ever blossom, ever ring,
Gentle, lucid, laughing spring !

CHICKAMAUGA.

This evening a shudder came o'er me
    As I tramped this broad battlefield o'er,
And thought of the feet that before me
    Had hurried there dripping with gore.

I thought of each struggle so gory
    With thousands that wrestled for might,

Each call on the soldier for glory
　　With the plea that he fought for the right.

The plain is a ruin of forest
　　And fort that depict the fierce fray ;
The plowshare, in efforts the poorest,
　　Would hide each grim vestige away.

Broken bayonets are seen at each fastness,
　　There molder the musket and blade ;
The graveyard bespeaks in its vastness
　　The havoc these relics have made.

I turned from the field as the shadows
　　Marked out the long lines of the foe,
To picture the orphans and widows,
　　And hearts yet unsoothed in their woe ;

The rattle of steel seemed to follow,
　　The guns from each rampart to speak,
I heard the poor sufferers hollo—
　　O fearful imagining, break !

SEQUACHEE.

A feathery cloud moves through the sky,
   Green velvet lawns spread to the west,
Waves play upon the wheat and rye,
   The partridge weaves her grassy nest.

The lucid corn extends its arms
   To catch the honey-dews that fall,
The gardens blush beneath their charms,
   The pea cocks dart about and squall.

From every hill a streamlet breaks,
   And rivers mirror back the scene ;
The shadowy wood with twitters wakes,
   And cattle wallow on the green.

Blue mountain peaks jut up beyond
   The paradise that spreads between ;
Some fairy must have waved his wand,
   And built this happy, heavenly scene.

ROLLICKING RIVERS.

Ho! broad is the space that divides us,
　　The rivers that laugh the day through ;
Ho! rough are the crags I've been crossing,
　　They hide your sweet home from my view.

Though broad be this space that divides us,
　　No spirit so kind it assures ;
Though wide be these rollicking rivers
　　They mirror no home like to yours.

'Tis a memory loved that goes with me,
　　Of days in our tramps through your groves ;
'Tis a blessing to dream thus forever
　　Of things that my spirit so loves.

Then remember, sweet lady, though parted,
　　I dream of you, love you the same ;
What though there be spaces between us,
　　I know they exist but in name.

Come nights with your chill, dewy mantle,
　　Gleam dimly, ye stars, from above,
This world has a charm while yet lingers
　　A hope of my old, dearest love.

Roll laughing or mad, ye deep rivers,
　　And spread, ye broad plains, as you will,
You cannot divide me and loved ones,
　　My spirit will live with them still.

THE OLD TENNESSEE.

Shadowed by mountains that play with the cloud,
   Marked in your course by the gray rocks of time,
Dark, rushing waters that sprays often shroud,
   River, the road that you tread is sublime !

Gathering the bright, sportive streams as you move,
   River, you've parted the heights that oppose ;
Leaving the hills far behind I so love,
   Through valleys romantic your rapid flood goes.

Borne on your bosom your march I've pursued,
   Seen you united with floods not your own ;
Doubting, how often my hopes you've renewed !
   River, I love you for times that are gone.

Spring ushers in and your long fertile vales,
   River, outbloom all the rest of the land ;
Autumn returns, but your corn never fails,
   Loaded with nuts here your tall hickories stand.

Angling. how often I've rowed o'er your tide !
   Sporting how oft I have known your embrace !
Often have stood on your steep, pearly side,
   Viewing the moon as it danced on your face.

Mirroring back the grand scenes where you rove,
   River unbounded, flow ever as free !
Others may choose what they will for their home,
   Give *me* a home by the old Tennessee !

"Shadowed by mountains that play with the cloud,
Marked in your course by the gray rocks of time."

—Page 18.

GO, LOVE, TO THE WORLD.

Go, love, to the world with your beauty,
    And seek what you find not in me ;
They, too, may make loving a duty—
    I know that you long to be free.

Go, love, to another while youthful,
    Your love-lighted visage will win,
But know he can ne'er be as truthful,
    As constantly kind as I've been.

Give your heart to his fires as a fuel,
    As fiercely he joined in the strife ;
But. darling, remember how cruel
    You break the dear dream of my life !

Go, leave me the world's cold derision,
    They cannot reprove me too much,
And learn that your hopes are a vision,
    A bubble that bursts with your touch.

Go, learn that deceivers are many,
    The faithful and loving are few ;
When a friend you have found not in any,
    Come back and I still will be true.

So when in life's desert you welter
　　With hopes that are mangled and low,
Remember in me there's a shelter
　　Awaiting your pleasure as now.

Now wandering by Jordan's cold river
　　I give up the hope I once knew ;
How peaceful my days had they never
　　Been crossed by a heart so untrue !

I'll strive not to grieve though you sever
　　The cords that my heart fondly wove,
'Tis better to lose you than never
　　To have had the sweet pleasure of love.

Then go to the world with your graces,
　　You've a cloudless and beautiful view ;
You'll meet with more lovable faces,
　　But never a spirit as true.

SUNNY EYES.

I cannot see your face by night
    When shine unveiled those lustrous spheres,
For in their fierce electric light
    They blind me, if not dimmed with tears ;
'Tis when a cloud envelops Jove
We scan the burning space above.

Sometimes, like Dido, I forget
    Those orbs cannot be looked upon,
So, venturing from my screening net,
    I fall to plead before the throne,
But, just as when I view the sun,
I shield my blinded eyes and run.

So pass the years, I cannot view
    Those dazzling lights but when a tear
Flows o'er them its obstructing hue
    To dim the immortal phase they wear ;
Then weep to break the blinding light,
And soothe me with unbroken sight.

GUSHING HEART.

Say, whither will a finite start
  In search of words that prove
A gushing, gushing, gushing heart
  That gushes o'er with love ?

No, tell me not mid severed thought
  Such truths as this may shine,
There never was a fondness wrought
  In time as true as mine.

No, never mortal love's its name
  By time and space subdued,
Mine is a bright celestial flame,
  Though bursting yet renewed ;

For henceforth when I wish I know,
  Though space be rolled between,
Before me as in heaven will glow
  Your beauty sweet, serene.

Then let this sphere of nature part,
  No changes can it prove ;
In heaven I'll own this gushing heart
  Is wholly, truly love.

" bright, peaceful homes reflected here
In rivers that seem but the sky."—Page 25.

TENNESSEE.

Resplendent sun with glorious light,
    Whose parting leaves the evening lull
To stud the sky with stars so bright,
    'Tis here you are most beautiful.

O crystal streams from mountain's peak,
    Whose waters every sport assure,
And thousand springs from hills that break,
    The world has nothing else as pure !

O beauteous vales that spread between
    These mountain heights and picture bliss,
Fanned by a breeze from skies serene,
    There's not another scene like this !

Bright, peaceful homes reflected here
    In rivers that seem but the sky,
Shadowed by trees and rocks as dear,
    No lovelier prospects meet the eye !

Dear, sighing groves, I want to find
    Your shadows by some sparkling brook,
And, basking in the cooling wind,
    Give up the eve to pen and book !

I want to find a water-mill
    That rumbles far up some ravine,

For there I know the blissful thrill
  Of solitude in peace serene.

I love to know the peace that shrouds
  These fields where armies spent their might,
Or walk among the floating clouds
  Of Lookout Mountain's dizzy height.

There's not a dream the age records
  Of iron wheels that banish space,
There's not a blessing earth affords,
  But in its glory here we trace.

Young Spring, 'tis here your sweetest stroke
  Dissolves in lovelier depths I see ;
Each flowery bank and shadowy oak
  Affords a paradise for me.

Oft by the noisy water-fall
  I view the tides that whirl and seethe,
Or listen to the pewit's call
  While strolling where the willows wreathe.

My Tennessee, from east to west
  Yours is the fairest earth imparts,
There's not another land so blest
  With pretty girls and noble hearts.

O Tennessee, the rich and great,
  Forever thus your triumphs be !
Let others seek some other state,
  I'll live and die in Tennessee.

LOVED ONES AFAR.

On the soft gleaming sands of the sea-shore to night
    I wander and gaze on the sea ;
The full moon on high, with her arrowy light,
    Gilds nature with beauty for me.

The cool, balmy breezes come whispering along
    With the billows that thunder ashore ;
The mocking-bird, piping his varied song,
    Is heard above Ocean's loud roar.

Wave rises and rushes to fall on the shore
    Where its comrade soon dashes its spray ;
Like armies they come, while the columns before
    Forever are melting away.

I gather the sea-shells for loved ones afar,
    From whose kindness I long have been gone ;
They kiss me and whisper, " Wherever you are
    Forget not the hearts yet your own."

I love the deep ocean, the sea-shore, this light
    That gilds the broad prospect for me,
But I'd rather be back with those loved ones to-night
    Than gaze on this beauteous sea.

"The cool, balmy breezes come whispering along,
With the billows that thunder ashore." —Page 27.

DEAF AT LAST.

Sweetheart whom I thought sincere,
Who my pleadings stooped to hear,
    Is deaf at last;
Though I speak with brazen throat,
Though I use the timbrel's note,
    She hears no blast.

Roarings from the dark, deep sea,
Matins from the citron tree
    And apricot,
All a lover's sad lament
With the pine-tree's moan, I've sent,—
    She hears them not.

Jessamine's from the hammocks deep,
Golden fruits in bounteous heap,
    And shells from seas;
Plumes from wild-birds timid, brave.
Views of beauteous lakes, I gave,—
    They failed to please.

Oh! the times my muse implored,
Sweetheart yet the more ignored;
    When parted we

Said she, " I'll neglect no more,
'Tween us though as ne'er before
    Should roll the sea."

Favored thus I trusting roved,
She again has faithless proved ;
    My sweetheart, gone !
Never did I b'lieve a breast
Where so many virtues rest
    Was wanting one.

Walking 'lone on Flora's shore
I shall hear old Ocean's roar,
    And hope, erelong,
Happy, gentle, waking spring
Her remembered smiles will bring
    To land of song.

At the morning's golden gate
I, condemned to sigh and wait,
    Look o'er the sea ;
Spring with tidings flits along,
Waves roll in with smile and song,
    But none for me.

SOUL IN SONG.

Did not I see your fingers move
To notes that spoke in tones of love,
Rebound the living keys along,
Thus sweeping off my soul in song?
I gazed upon the instrument
And wondered not, its tones were lent,
I knew the melodies it spoke
Forth from your heavenly spirit broke
I knew the airs I heard it roll
Were as they lived within your soul;
I gazed upon your calm, fair face,
To day my eyes' loved resting-place,
I knew a soul was peering through
Those tender eyes of ocean hue,
That pictured in your angel mien,
Was most of heaven earth had seen.
Each shadow drew its length away,
The twilight grew as bright as day,
My eyes were fixed immovably
Upon the soul that spoke so gay;
If in my heart grief had a place
Your music ravaged every trace.

    Dear lady, strike those keys once more,
And let me know my raptures o'er,
 No sweeter pain I ever knew
Than when your music through me flew.

AHAPOPKA.

(One of Florida's largest lakes.)

Ahapopka, laughing sea,
   Mirror of your shores and sky,
Take these simple flowers from me,
   Never more you'll greet my eye!

I have stemmed your rippled tide,
   Laughed upon your placid face,
I have slumbered by your side,
   Sported in your cool embrace.

Now those happy days are o'er,
   Soon I quit your sunny isles,
Sad to day I walk your shore,
   Take my tears instead of smiles.

Lonely is my sable bower,
   I have left its silent room ;
It has not a bird or flower
   That can cheer a heart of gloom.

All your beauteous shores afford
   Gave my life a happier birth ;
Where are scenes like these restored ?
   Where is heaven so much on earth ?

You are beautiful, O sea !
   More than words like mine can tell ;
Still your charms will live with me,
   Ahapopka, fare you well !

WALK IN FLORIDA.

Zephyr flitting o'er the seas,
  Wooing e'er this land of spring,
Zephyr with the spicy breeze,
  Fan me with your cooling wing!

Kiss me! I was late relieved
  From old Winter's icy clutch;
Kiss me! I am not deceived,
  'Tis your lips' delightful touch.

Day and night sweet notes I hear,
  Filling every citrus grove;
Genial spirits hold me near,
  Angels greet me where I rove.

Thousand lakes embraced with flowers
  Glad in every walk, my eyes;
Golden fruits and cooling bowers,
  Beckon as the morning flies.

Water-fowls of beauteous plume,
  Fishes sportman's arts decoy,
Blooming groves with heaven's perfume,
  Make this land a scene of joy.

2

GONE TO THE BLEST.

This day they have buried my treasure
    Where oft we have playfully trod,
My beauty beyond mortal measure,
    Too soon to be pressed by the sod.

O light in the lovely to-morrow,
    Refracted but beauteous ray!
You leave us the burdening sorrow,
    The darkness that follows the day.

Too bleak was the breath of December
    To nurture a dahlia so pure;
You have gone to the blest, but remember
    You leave us the brunt to endure.

The miscreant Death, ere he prest you,
    Concealed not his sighs as he stood,
But the angels rejoiced and caressed you,
    To give you the home of the good.

You have gone from the sinful and fleeting,
    Where specious Temptation allures;
In heaven will next be our meeting
    If our lives are as perfect as yours.

You have gone to a world where your equals
   And likes your companions will be ;
Where love is your life, and the sequels
   Of truth are the joys you will see.

You have gone from the suffering and dying,
   Where love is born but to be crossed ;
But think of the hearts that are sighing,
   And *mine* that is wounded the most.

O lady, beloved but immortal,
   Turn back but to soothe the bereft !
Look, love, from your spiritual portal,
   As we walk in the light you have left !

Good-bye, my beloved beyond measure !
   Your pean is heard from above ;
Your smile that was most of our pleasure
   Now beams on the angels of love.

Good-bye ! but the laurel shall ever
   Bloom over your dust as in May,
And know from our loving hearts never
   Will fade the first memory away.

AT HER GRAVE.

I heard that the Lord of all creatures
  Had taken my angel He gave ;
I hastened to gaze on her features,
  But only returned to her grave.

The breezes were cold and outspoken,
  And freshly upturned was the sod ;
I stood by the palings there broken
  And bowed to the will of my God.

I felt that the blow had bereft me
  Of most of this world I have found ;
The evening departed and left me
  To weep by the desolate mound.

But why should I linger here giving
  Up most of my evenings to pine ?
I know that my loved one is living
  In a world that is brighter than mine.

A memory sweet never leaves me
  Of life with a heart all my own ;
'Tis only her absence that grieves me—
  My life is so cheerless and lone.

I'll wait till this journey is over,
  Though often bereavements must come ;
I know that my lost I'll recover
  To love in the spiritual home.

ECHOING VALES.

Dear girl, in the vale where your lovable form
    Was sheltered in earlier years,
Where we greeted the sunshine or breasted the storm
    To mingle our blessings and fears ;
Where we rowed o'er the river that glided along
    With a rollicking laugh ever new,
Or squandered the moments in transport and song, —
    I count o'er my memories to you.

Here stands the gray crag that we mounted to view
    The landscape before us that lay ;
Above it the sky bends as cloudless and blue
    As it did in our happiest May.
The skiff that we paddled here rests on the shore,
    But time has corroded its chain ;
The gunwales are broken, the burdens it bore
    Perhaps it will bear ne'er again.

Here the cataract falls, and its thunders are heard
    On the mountain and thorn-covered moor ;
Here often we strayed and we spoke not a word,
    But by gesture, so deafening the roar.

"Here stands the gray crag that we mounted to view
The landscape before us that lay;"—Page 37.

Here circle the eddies and bubble the boils
    Where we waited and angled of yore :
Here the old water-wheel with its burden still toils,
    The mill rocks and groans as before.

Here rises the dwelling that sheltered your head,
    But its rooms have been silent for years ;
The beauteous soul that adorned it has fled--
    I view the old cottage through tears.
The fences are broken, the lilies are gone
    Your eyes so delighted to view ;
Here Loneliness sits on the fountain's cold stone,
    Day and night she is mourning for you.

The "too whoo" of the owl echoes loud through this vale,
    Like our pleasures the day softly dies,
Now comes on the breezes the night-bird's sad wail,
    And the moon drops her light from the skies.
How pensive to stand in this valley and see
    Sable night spread her mantle abroad !
My comrade removed, here is left but for me
    Wandering love and a crag-covered road.

MONTEZUMA'S SEA.

Looking o'er this rippled sea
  Which recedes beyond my sight,
Tired of books that load my knee,
  Tired of sea-gulls in their flight,—

I'm reflecting on the time
  This broad water holds me here,
Burning neath a sultry clime,
  Homesick though my tent is near.

Backward moves the moaning tide,
  All the sea-birds herald night;
Go, you ocean, deep and wide!
  I must leave you while there's light.

But to-morrow where I move
  Far from this resplendent view,
Oh! my heart will ache with love
  And my sighs be all for you.

FARE YOU WELL.

Fare you well! may peace attend you
　　Through the vale I leave behind,
May each wounded heart befriend you
　　Though your every thought's unkind.
Though we part, my prayers will greet you
　　Through the years you bid me go ;
Should the fiercest fortune meet you
　　Still those blessings you will know.

Oh ! the anxious hopes that cheered me,
　　Thrills so long my sweetest pang ;
Oh ! the pledges that endeared me
　　Fall to ashes where they sprang.
How my pining heart has loved you,
　　Weltering at your feet a slave !
Your reproachful look has proved
　　False to every vow you gave.

When a careless child I sought you
　　Straying through your woodland wild,
Little treasured gifts I brought you,
　　Which you took and always smiled.

Where no curious eye could greet us
　　Pledged we then we'd never part,
What e'er be the fates that meet us
　　Each would hold the other's heart.

Like the morning skies that greet me
　　But ere noon with clouds is black,
Your dear love that used to meet me
　　Quits its early beaten track.
Fare you well! the hearts that love you
　　Fall beneath the cruel blow ;
Though my kindness may not move you,
　　Soon my sorrow you shall know.

STROLL IN THE SOUTHLAND.

From the wild Appalachians long lost in the haze,
I stroll in the Southland through long sunny days.

I passed the dense heathers of Cumberland heights ;
The deer bounded by me, and their eyes were great lights.

I left the Warito* whose smiles yet I trace,
But stooped in my wonder and kissed its bright face.

I've gone from the fountains that gush from your hills
To bathe in the seas that my heart ever fills.

Removed from my loved ones I stroll o'er this strand,
Where summer forever is queen of the land ;

Where palm and the cypress encircle the lakes,
And this glittering pontchartrain of laughter partakes ;

Where gay birds unwearied flit over the scene,
And the gray, friendless spider is weaving his screen.

*Indian name of Cumberland River.

Each prospect that greets me as daily I rove,
Brings back to my memory the home that I love.

These waters unbounded go sporting along,
And wake in my bosom a volume of song.

My days are a joy in the rapturous wood,
And my nights even more as I float on the flood.

Could a shadow of grief ever dawn in this place,
To darken the sunlight of beauty I trace?

Oh! no, but when fancy transforms each dear spot,
And pictures my home where I know it is not.

SPIRIT IN HEAVEN.

O Spirit whose home is celestial,
  Removed from this censure and strife
To pleasures unknown to the bestial,
  Think of those in the outskirts of life.

We know you still live and about you
  Are cares for your happier birth,
But still we are grieved for without you
  What pleasure affords this old earth ?

Spring bursts from its confines and glitters
  As bright as the morning we met;
The prospect, though gay, but imbitters,
  And life is o'ercast with regret.

I seek the green woodland at vesper,
  Where birds at their nest weaving ply ;
I think of your soft, loving whisper,
  And quit the dear scene with a sigh.

I list to the brooklet's low mumbling,
   The voices I hear seem to say,
That fate is so cruel and humbling,
   This world had not tired of your stay.

By streamlets more lovely you wander,
   And landscapes sublimer you see ;
With brighter companions you squander
   The evenings you once gave to me.

I know that the beauties that greet you
   Lead you far in that love-lighted place ;
But wait, only wait till we meet you,
   And those grandeurs together we'll trace.

Yes, wait at the entrance to heaven,
   Our canvas is soon to be furled ;
When by one tempest more we are driven
   We'll meet in the spiritual world.

SONNET TO SPRING.

Still frolics Spring, the fields with spikes are strown,
  The mumbling brooklets through the meadows flow,
  The mock-birds trill, the busy planters go ;
Good bye to Winter since his frosts are gone :
I stroll among the rugged cliffs alone
  At eve to see the sunset's dying glow,
  Or troll in rapids where the blushing bow
Of Iris bends above me as my own.
O lovely scene, beloved delightful Spring,
  Reward of four months' suffering in the frost!
We laugh forever 'neath your verdant wing
  But sigh forever when your smiles are lost ;
Sear Autumn may have pleasures yet to bring,
  But flowers and sunshine children love the most.

CUPID'S CAPTIVE.

I say not that I love you, still
    From every sigh's repulsion
You see my senses and my will
    Are struggling in convulsion.
My anxious glances when I rise
    To pay each benediction,
Discover surely to your eyes,
    This homage is no fiction.

It is enough, I'll plead no more
    In love's replete advances ;
My spirit begs for only your
    Benignant smiles and glances.
Have mercy! 'tis no fiendish call,
    I ask it through emotion ;
From that exalted summit fall,
    To bathe in love's pure ocean.

OOTHTANAKEE.

(Falls of Taylor's Creek. Tenn.)

Hovering here excluding day
Ever hangs this cloud of spray,
Through the trees the tempest howls,
Far below the water scowls ;
Here a tempest cleaves its way
Through this fissure night and day,
Leaping from the cliffs around
Fall the streams with deafening sound,
Dancing, sparkling, wild they come
Bursting into mist and foam :
Sometimes, when the vapors sway,
Struggles through a beam of day,
Then in mists again immured
Thus this grandeur is obscured.
Through the cloud that wraps the scene
Iris bends her lovely mien,
While above the mantling spray
Glow the silver shafts of day.
     Where these dark abutments stand
Smile and frown go hand in hand,
Beauties greet you, yet beware,
Dark, deep chasms await you there.
Oothtanakee in despair
Sought these cliffs to end his care,
On the hungry rocks below
Broke his cumbrous load of woe.

" Beauties greet you, yet beware,
    Dark, deep chasms await you there."   Page 49.

BLISSFUL DREAMS.

Love, may I lay my head to rest
Once more upon your snowy breast,
There near the heart I love the most
Let all things else in dreams be lost ?

While pillowed thus my spirit eyes
Ope softly on elysian skies ;
Yes, sleeping there as evening dies,
To heaven in dreams my spirit flies.

For waking oft you fondly wait.
I wake, am still at heaven's gate ;
How fond the love, how sweet the rest,
To kiss and slumber on your breast !

Then greet me at your generous home,
To know your love again I come,
There through your sweet lips to absorb
The soul that guides me like an orb.

I'll have no need to turn away
In spirit from this realm of clay,
To seek in other worlds the bliss
That thrills me in your soothing kiss.

Still in your youthful mien I trace
The beauty of an angel's face,
So heaven, instead of far away,
Here daily beams upon my way.

When sleeping I shall dream of you,
The most of heaven I ever knew,
And waking, I'll again caress
The form I so much love to bless.

The time approaches, love, when we
Again those happy hours shall see,
Gaze fondly in each love-lit eye
To kiss and kiss and kiss *good bye*!

Oh! no we never more can part
Lest each will take the other's heart,
Thus treasured, though apart we rove,
To still as fondly, truly love.

Erelong the mountain's frozen crest
My feet must press as oft they've prest,

There with old Winter's chilling powers
To wrestle as in former hours.

Too soon between us Ocean's roar
Will clash as it has not before,
And I must give your kindly home
For clouded skies and salt sea-foam.

Although I go with footsteps fleet
My heart is lowly at your feet,
Though cruel fates my life control
My love's as lasting as my soul.

When on the sea my head shall rest
I'll think it is your heaving breast,
And when sweet sleep and dreams are given
I'll know not but I'm with my heaven.

HOPES IN ASHES.

Yes, I know the hopes I cherish
  Here must end,
Joys I thought would never perish
  Here must end ;
Oh ! the grave must hold my pleasures !
Place the sod above my treasures
  Where they fall.

Oh ! I'm lonely weeping, sighing
  O'er my fate,
Oh ! my heart is wilting, dying
  O'er my fate ;
Your fair hands have dug the fissure,
Mine must lie beneath the pressure
  Evermore !

Now your angel form has left me
  Dying here,
Your sweet smile of life bereft me
  Dying here ;
Never more on earth to meet you,
Not to think in heaven I'll greet you,
  Darling love !

Fare you well! but yet I welter
    At your door,
Gone forever is the shelter
    Of your love ;
Yet, though weltering, don't deride me,
Broad, dark distance must divide me
    And your love.

Let your elm-tree lift its moaning
    Where I fall,
Let your mock-bird sing till dawning
    At my grave ;
I'll be truly blest in dying
If you'll woo me, kiss me lying
    At your door.

BE MINE IN HEAVEN.

It seems that I had fixed my heart
   On one some less repulsive,
It seems, as fruitless years depart,
   I'd break this spell convulsive.

Not so, my love springs up anew
   And blooms as spring-time finds me,
My soul is ever fixed on you,
   Nor Time nor Fate unbinds me.

Yes, as the seasons decades bring,
   Take hopes I cherished early,
My love blooms in unfading spring
   And furls your breast more nearly.

Oh ! what a pleasure that will be,
   To know I'll love forever,
In dreams your beauteous face to see,
   And break those visions never !

To know, though never more be given
　　On earth, a time to bless you,
I'll love you when we meet in heaven
　　And still as fondly bless you.

But what a stunning, murderous blow
　　If in those realms elysian
Your lovely smiles I did not know
　　In truth or kindred vision !

Let years be numberless or few,
　　Forgive the oft told story,
How quick they'd go if I but knew
　　You'd wed me, love. in glory !

Then though my tree of hope is sear,
　　Its toppling crest is riven,
Speak, love, and make me happy here,
　　Say you'll be mine in heaven !

WILD PIPER.

I hear an orchestra's sweet pleading
  This eve as the shadows grow long,
I hear the wild piper's loud carol
  Converting the vale into song.

The soft breeze is rife with the flute notes
  That ring from the mountain away;
They come as bright dreams of the parted,
  The joys of a happier day.

WORLD'S EXPOSITION.

(New Orleans, Feb, 1885.)

Summary of earth, lost in your depths I rove!
  Gleanings from every age, from every clime!
I find each art, invention, age I love
  Mixed in one dazzling show, O scene sublime!

Why journey further? England, Egypt, Rome,
  Japan, France, Greece and China lavish here

Their products, and old Mexico's at home,
   But Turks' and Arabs' pipes the ribbons wear.

Spreads here with careful hands our own fair land
   Her thousand cereals; well she may not blush :
Here stretches Georgia, yonder rises grand
   Vermont in marble, Kansas makes a rush.

My Tennessee well burdened answers " Here ! "
   In all but apples, I could eat her store ;
For corn and peas a label she should wear,
   Such beets and 'tatoes never hit this shore !

Here's Florida in thousand different woods,
   And fruits as numerous as her crocodiles ;
There sits old California with competing goods,
   Wreathing her sunburnt face with broadcast smiles.

They turn us in at 10 A. M., all day
   We jostle thousands, shove our way from Spain
Across to China, through the States, and stay
   A while at Yeddo waiting for the train.

In pottery I believe old Venice wins,
   Give Mexico a button for her beans,
Texas should have a cracker for her skins,
   For Carnivals the prize is New Orleans'!

THORNLESS FLOWERS.

Let the rose without the thorn
  Line your path as never mine,
Hither sweetest joys be borne
  While on guard may angels shine.

Let the storms that press my brow
  Lull their rage ere reaching you,
Let the waves that beat my prow
  Nearing yours their peace renew.

Be each dearth of hope for me,
  Famine for my lips alone,
I am always blest to see
  Yours a pleasure not my own.

MEMORIES OF GEORGIA.

From the dark Cohuttah Mountains
Where Cotakah and Ellijah
Clasp their tiny hearts in wedlock,
Down the reedy Coosawattee
Till it weds the Connesauga,
Down the rocky Oostanaula,
Through the trodden field Resaca,
Till the Etowah and Coosa
Mingled with the Tallapoosa,
And the glorious Alabama
Gave me to the Montezuma, —
Oh! my heart so much exulted
I was weary once with pleasure.
In the vale of Oothcaloga
Waved the harvest, sang the plowman,
And the peaks of Allatoona
Echoed back the dying numbers,
And the yellow Chattahoochee
Rolled its majesty before me,
Till it met the Thronateeska,
Made the Appalachicola.

All alone by the Ocmulgee
In the shadows of the pine-trees
Oft I fished away the evenings,
Rowed upon its smooth, deep waters
To the sandy, dark Oconee,
Rested on the Altamaha,
Drifted to the Great Ohoopee.

Once I loved the Withlocoochee,
Strolled among its cool, dense hammocks,
But the laughing Allapaha
Won me with its brighter lupines,
And the little Suwanoochee
Lured me to the old Suwanee.

Once I sought the swift Tallulah,
Till it wedded the Chattooga,
Followed on the clear Tugalo
To the beautiful Savannah,
Bathed my bark in the Kiokee,
Sheltered in the lap of Uchee,
Rested on the far Ogeechee.

Far beyond the Ocklokonee
And the gentle Okopilco,
Where no more the Kinchafoonee
Leads us to the Thronateeska,
And the moaning Ichawaynochaway,
Spread the breaks of Okefenokee.
Once I floundered in its jungles
As I rambled in the Southland,

"But a gentle ignis-fatuus
Led me back to the Satilla."—Page 64.

But a gentle ignis-fatuus
Led me back to the Satilla.
     Good-bye, Georgia! yet your Soquee
Fills my heart like Auchee Hachee,
And the sobbing Tobesofkee
Calls my thoughts to Towaliga.
O the shades of Appalachee!
They are loved as the Tocoa,
And your Cannauchee reminds me
Of my Tennessee's Hiwassee,
Of the playful stream Sequachee.

BRIGHT BE YOUR DAYS.

Peaceful and bright be your days,
  Gilded with hope's silver beam,
Freed from each gathering haze
  Be your journey one beautiful dream.

Sweet be the roses that line
  Your pathway while blossom the trees,
Soft be the clasp of the vine
  That holds your young heart in its wreathes.

Long be the spring you will know
  The brightest the world ever knew,
Hushed be each breath that would flow
  Opposed to a vision like you.

Your road is a pageant more bright
  Than earth, so we follow your wake :
But, oh! give us peace in your might,
  Be gentle with hearts that you break !

'Tis a meteor passing I know,
   All the stars have grown dim in the blaze
You give to our world a bright glow
   But *my* heart feels the most while we gaze.

O light that has ravaged the world,
   Comet drawing the orbs in your wake,
O spirit of beauty unfurled,
   Be kind to the hearts that you break

SAY, DO YOU, DARLING.

Say, do you darling, when you milk
    Your gentle cows or rope the calf.
Or sweep away the spider's silk,
    But think of me sometimes and laugh ?

Say, when you slap the beds about
    Or fling their covers out to sun,
A moment, love, forget to pout
    To think of me and days of fun.

When bending o'er the heated stove
    You roll the roasting coffee free,
Or when the biscuit pan you shove,
    Think so you've often done for me.

But when you splash the wash-tub, dear,
    With dripping clothes and soapy hands,
With bonnet flapped and dress you wear,
    I know your beauty most commands.

But when you pick the stately goose
    That kicks and screams at every blow,

Be merciful and turn him loose,
   Just think I would not treat *you* so.

How beautiful your evenings, love,
   For covering apples from the dews,
To give each romping child a shove
   And walk the porch without your shoes!

Do for me, as your chickens, care!
   I saw a hawk once make his swoop,
But you with gentle hands were there
   And put them in their little coop.

But when you're picking beans, beware!
   The stinging-worm's a sneaking foe;
Some playful lizard, hiding there,
   Might set you screaming " *snake*!" you know.

So, darling, still as useful be,
   And make your home a cloudless noon;
At table place a plate for me,
   For I'll be there to help you soon.

LOST IN FLORIDA.

Tuskeneha, tell me, guide,
  Where we are, we perish here !
Tempests gather far and wide,
  Thunders grate upon my ear.

What a grand, terrific light
  Flashes through this wilderness !
Yet each blaze that breaks the night
  Adds no hope in our distress

Through the fan-palms crocodiles
  Seek the pathway where we grope ;
Greeted by their hungry smiles,
We may bid adieu to hope.

'Mong these breaking, crashing trees
  Who would tremble not with dread ?
Near us break the angry seas,
  Here the clouds their vengeance shed.

Gladly would we say good night
  To this flashing, swaying scene ;
No, we wander here till light
  Tears away the sable screen.

Indian's hut perhaps is near
  Hajo, speak your signal call ;
Nothing but these hammocks hear,
  Where no human footsteps fall.

Yet may not a shelter be
  In this tangled forest found ?
Yonder, lo ! an orange-tree
  Spreads its sheltering leaves around.

Guided by the lightning's blaze,
  Marshes, miring sands, we press ;
Chilled by rains and salt-sea sprays,
  Thus we tramp this wilderness.

STORM AT SEA.

How many weary days must come
  Before I see your face,
Before I greet you at your home
  And know your loved embrace !

My bark is waiting, love, to fly
  Across the waters wide,
But Montezuma's Sea is high,
  I cannot stem the tide.

How fast the mountain billows come,
  Tossed wildly by the gale !
While madly thus they heap their foam
  No. seaman spreads his sail.

I would not now forsake this shore
  Were tempests half as high ;
I never saw such seas before,
  Such blazes through the sky.

But by the favoring smiles of Heaven.
  Which ever mine may be,
Ere one brief season more be given
  We'll meet beyond the sea.

LAND OF FLOWERS.

———

If far Sahara be a land
Of dancing heat and burning sand,
Where all the beauty nature yields
Has long since withered from the fields,
Sahara is not here, this place
Assumes a brighter, lovelier face.
Here are the crystal lakes that smile
And mirror back each flowery isle,
Here grow the palms and hammocks green,
Old Winter does not change the scene,
Bay, live-oak. cypress, pine we view.
Magnolias claim attention, too,   .
Here softly fans the cool sea-breeze,
All day it moans among the trees,
The orange, citron, guava, date,
The pains to gather only wait,
Limes, lemons, cocoas, grape fruits, figs,
Here swing upon the living twigs,
And May, delightful May, has made
Her home forever in this shade.
A thousand birds of plumage gay
Are swimming on each liquid way,

These citrus groves the whole day long
Are ringing with the voice of song;
Here is the sea, the playful sea,
Which always had a charm for me,
Upon whose sands I often stand
And watch the billows kiss the land:
My sail I spread before the breeze
That wafts me on with speed and ease—
How truly blest is life to be
A citizen beside this sea?
We want an artist here to trace
The beauties all these lakes embrace,
We want a poet here to sing
To glory this abode of Spring;
But had the Fates been pleased to own
I had a right to music's throne,
These warblers soon would hush their throats
And list to stranger, sweeter notes,
Or could I wield the painter's brush
The canvas I would boldly touch,
And all the beauties that are here
In other climes would re-appear.

OCKLAWAHA.

(A tributary of the St. Johns' Fla.)

Quit the North, you sportive rover,
Fields perfumed with blooming clover,
Quit the city's rushing, jeering,
Mountain rocks that boast in peering,
Quit Niagra, Minnehaha,
Seek the brakes of Ocklawaha,
Seek the hammocks of a river
Where old Winter's fingers never
 Plucked the flowers.
Sol may rise and pour his blazes
Where Kissimmee's flood amazes,
Far beneath these dark recesses
His sear heat no more oppresses,
Cruel Care no more distresses,
Thoughts are fixed on scenes embowering,
Cypress, palms, magnolias towering,
Mid the tangles many a wonder
Half your former griefs will sunder,
Further, deeper, penetrating

Where bright birds are ever prating
　　Fly the hours.
Part the hammock. seek the river,
There the sunbeams gayly quiver
In the shadows deep and lasting,
There no tempests loud and blasting
Break the waters' gentle slumbers,
But the mock-bird's varied numbers
　　Float serene.

DARK WARRIORS ARE WHERE?

I went to the vale of the echoing Fred,
   The walls of dark granite affronted the cloud;
They were blackened with smoke, but the warriors had
      fled;
   There thundered the cascade, and spray was its shroud.

I turned to the caverns, the inmates had fled,
   The twilight recesses I ventured to probe,
But on the damp pavements where revels had sped
   Old Loneliness sat in his odious robe.

The warriors' grim ensigns of victory hung there,
   I viewed each strange trace of a people and sighed;
On leaving I spoke, "The dark warriors are where?"
   "Dark warriors are where?" all the caverns replied.

CRYSTAL CAVERNS.

I ween old Jupiter to-night
Will thunder from his heavenly height,
As eight o'clock repeats its jolt
He'll turn loose every thunder-bolt,
Eolus rolls his winds along,
Big clouds of dust are in the throng ;
Why does not Neptune interfere
To check this wrath of Jupiter ?
No, let it storm till mountains tilt,
Of black-gum logs my shanty's built.
Asleep or 'wake I don't know which,
At Panama I dig a ditch,
Pshaw, Clio, such a dev'lish dream !
Things are not often what they seem ;
Here through this port-hole let us view
The lightning's flashing, dazzling hue ;
The clouds are empty, not a drop
Of rain has struck my shanty's top !
Look, yonder where the thunders grate
A mountain lays its ponderous weight,
There is a palace under ground,
How tired the feet that tramp its round !

Crawling through holes you reach each room,
Superbly dread you'll think the gloom.
Lately those silent depths I viewed,
The way with broken rocks was strewed ;
There many a column, scars revealing,
Rose from the floor and kissed the ceiling,
As many prostrate blocked the floor,
Destructive hands had gone before,
A thousand spears from overhead
Stuck through my heart a sense of dread ;
What grander scenes beneath the sun
Than caverns like this awful one ?
But let us quit this noted sight
To climb the mountain's dizzier height ;
Peaches are ripe, they dangle free,
A zephyr rustles every tree.
Back to this room, my tramping o'er,
Through musty volumes late I pore,
Sometimes the midnight strikes its gong
And finds me bent o'er prose or song.

SUNSET.

The sun goes down into the dappled sea.
 A fading, ruby glimmer marks his grave,
The dew-drops kiss the opening flowers, the bee
 Well freighted seeks its isle across the wave.

The breezes cease to fan the fisher's brow,
 The billows hush their thunders on the shore,
The weary bird grows silent in his bough,
 And nature whispers, " Sunset, day is o'er !"

.

www.ingramcontent.com/pod-product-compliance
Lightning Source LLC
Chambersburg PA
CBHW020326090426
42735CB00009B/1425